Christian Crafts
for Christmastime

Christian Crafts
for
Christmastime

By Kathy Ross
Illustrated by Sharon Lane Holm

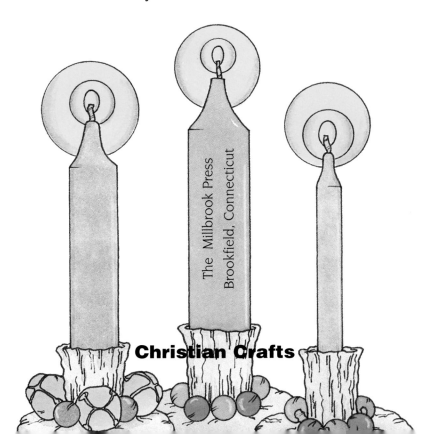

The Millbrook Press
Brookfield, Connecticut

Christian Crafts

For Beverly, who shares the spirit of the Christmas season with me.
K.R.

To Lee—my special, forever friend.
S.L.H.

With special thanks to Patti M. Hummel and the Benchmark Group

Library of Congress Cataloging-in-Publication Data
Ross, Kathy (Katharine Reynolds), 1948–
Christian crafts for Christmastime / by Kathy Ross;
illustrated by Sharon Lane Holm
p.   cm.
ISBN 0-7613-1620-5 (lib. bdg.) — ISBN 0-7613-1331-1 (pbk.)
1. Christmas decorations—Juvenile literature. 2. Bible crafts—Juvenile literature.
[1. Christmas decorations. 2. Handicraft.] I. Holm, Sharon Lane, ill. II. Title.
TT900.C4   R67496   2001
745.594'12—dc21   00--061634

Published by The Millbrook Press, Inc.
2 Old New Milford Road
Brookfield, Connecticut 06804
www.millbrookpress.com

Contents

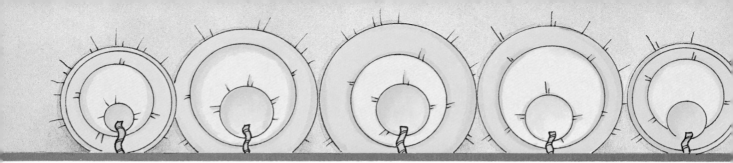

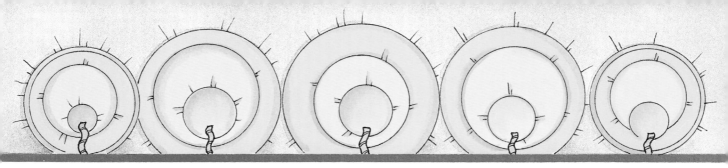

Introduction

The Christmas season is a time to celebrate the birth of Jesus. This book will help us to help our children focus on the real meaning of the holiday.

One proven way that children learn is by doing. CHRISTIAN CRAFTS FOR CHRISTMASTIME is a collection of hands-on projects that tell the story of Jesus' birth and reflect the love and joy that are the true spirit of Christmas. While working on the easy-to-make projects, children will learn about the Nativity and its meaning to the world. At the same time, the handmade gifts, cards, and ornaments they create will become tomorrow's treasured memories.

Take some time this season to enjoy sharing the Christmas spirit with your child.

Kathy Ross

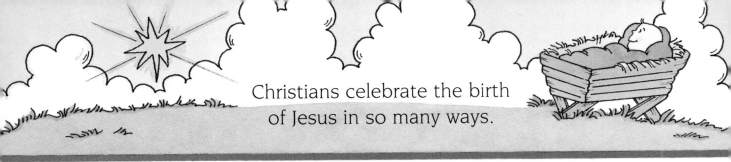

Christians celebrate the birth of Jesus in so many ways.

Nativity Panels

you need:

corrugated box cardboard

blue glue gel

scissors

ruler

plastic tape

gold glitter

gold spray paint

old jewelry

Christmas cards with scenes of the Christmas story

newspaper to work on

what you do:

1 Cut an arched window shape from the cardboard about 1 foot (30 cm) tall and 8 inches (20 cm) wide.

2 Cut two sidepieces from the cardboard, each about 8 inches square. Round off the outer corners of the two squares.

3 Cover the edges of all three pieces with the plastic tape.

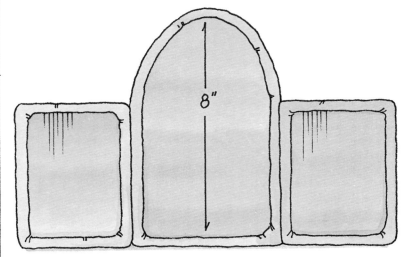

8"

4 Attach the two sidepieces to each side of the center unit with a strip of plastic tape down the back seam of each piece. This will allow the two sidepieces to swing forward to stand the triptych up.

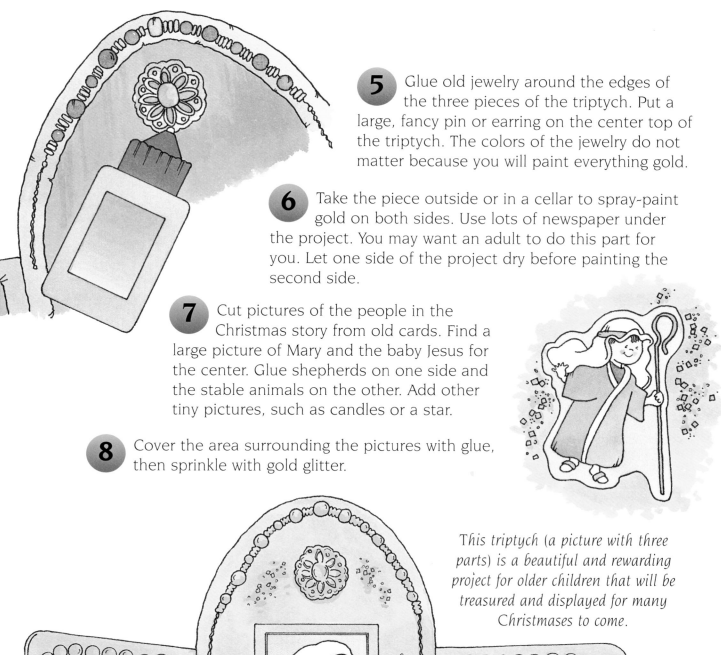

5 Glue old jewelry around the edges of the three pieces of the triptych. Put a large, fancy pin or earring on the center top of the triptych. The colors of the jewelry do not matter because you will paint everything gold.

6 Take the piece outside or in a cellar to spray-paint gold on both sides. Use lots of newspaper under the project. You may want an adult to do this part for you. Let one side of the project dry before painting the second side.

7 Cut pictures of the people in the Christmas story from old cards. Find a large picture of Mary and the baby Jesus for the center. Glue shepherds on one side and the stable animals on the other. Add other tiny pictures, such as candles or a star.

8 Cover the area surrounding the pictures with glue, then sprinkle with gold glitter.

This triptych (a picture with three parts) is a beautiful and rewarding project for older children that will be treasured and displayed for many Christmases to come.

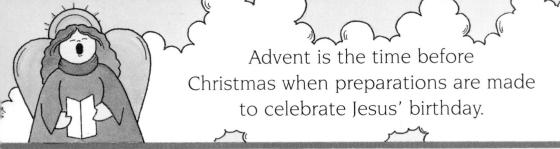

Advent is the time before
Christmas when preparations are made
to celebrate Jesus' birthday.

Angel Advent Calendar

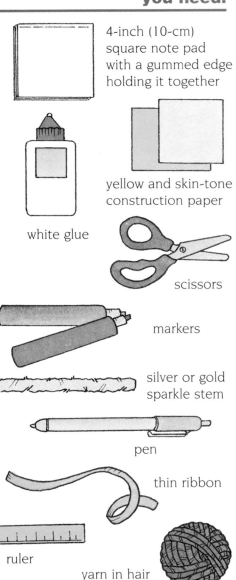

4-inch (10-cm)
square note pad
with a gummed edge
holding it together

yellow and skin-tone
construction paper

white glue

scissors

markers

silver or gold
sparkle stem

pen

thin ribbon

ruler

yarn in hair
color of your
choice

what you do:

1 Tear off a portion of the pad of paper with
enough pages so that there will be one page for
each day from the start of Advent until Christmas Eve.
Advent begins on the first of the four Sundays before
Christmas. Make sure you keep the pages held together by keeping the portion of the gummed binding that
holds the pages together intact when you remove the
stack of paper from the pad.

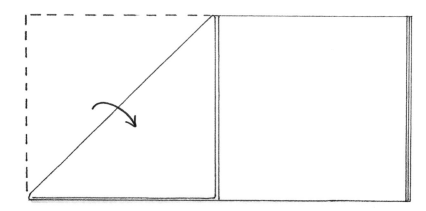

2 With the binding on the left, open the first page
of the pad like a book. Fold the top corner
down to the bottom corner to make each square a triangle. Fold each page this way except for the last one.
Fold the last page so that the fold is inside the book,
not outside. Fan the folded pages out and stand the
pages up to form the dress for the angel.

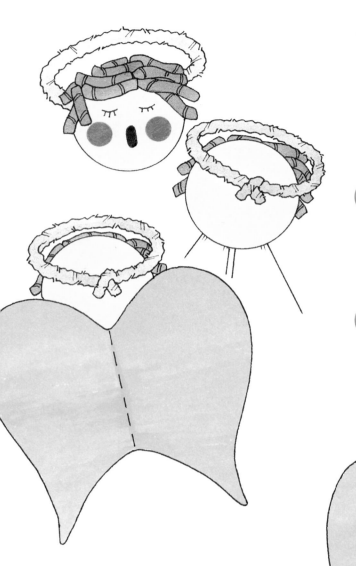

3 Cut a 2-inch (5-cm) circle for the head of the angel. Use the markers to give the angel a face. Glue on yarn bits for hair. Shape her halo from a 4-inch (10-cm) piece of the sparkle stem. Glue the halo on top of the head. Glue the bottom edge of the head to the back, top of the dress.

4 Fold a piece of the yellow paper in half. Cut a wing shape on the fold. Open the folded paper to get two wings attached at the center. Glue the wings to the back of the angel.

5 Cut a 6-inch (15-cm) length of the ribbon. Tie the ribbon into a bow. Glue the bow to the dress under the angel's chin.

Unfold each page of the angel dress and write down something special to do that day to prepare for the birthday of Jesus. It could be something like reading the Christmas story, arranging your doll friends to make a nativity scene, praying, or making cards or gifts.

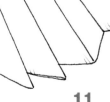

Christmas is a wonderful time
to decorate our homes for family
and friends.

Angel To-Do List

you need:

roll of adding-
machine tape

gold ribbon

pen

scissors

two tiny wiggle eyes

white glue

1-inch (2.5-cm)
Styrofoam ball

sparkle stem

yarn for hair

pink marker

red seed bead

silver foil cup-
cake wrapper

sticker
stars

ruler

white
tissue paper

what you do:

1 Cut a 2-foot (60-cm) length of gold ribbon. Thread one end through the center of the roll of adding-machine tape. Tie the two ends of the ribbon together in a bow to form a hanger for the roll of paper.

2 Cut a 10-inch (25-cm) square of white tissue paper for the dress of the angel.

3 Poke a hole partway through the Styrofoam ball using the writing end of the pen. This will be the head of the angel with the hole at the bottom of the head.

4 Glue the two wiggle eyes on the head. Glue on the red seed bead for a mouth. Cut some yarn bits and glue them to the top of the head for hair. Use the marker to give the angel pink cheeks.

5 Drape the center of the tissue square over the end of the pen, then cover the end with glue and slide the Styrofoam ball head over the glue-covered end of the pen.

6 Cut a 3-inch (8-cm) piece of sparkle stem. Wrap the two ends around each other to form a halo for the angel. Glue the halo to the top of the head.

7 Fold the foil cupcake wrapper in half. Cut the folded wrapper in half to make two wings for the angel. Glue the wings to the back of the angel with one sticking out on each side.

8 Trim around the bottom of the tissue dress so that it is even with the tip of the pen. Decorate the tissue dress with sticker stars.

9 Cut an 18-inch (46-cm) length of ribbon. Thread one end through the center of the paper roll. Bring the end around the front of the paper roll and tie it to the ribbon so that a long piece is left hanging down. Slide the resulting knot inside the center of the paper roll to hide it.

10 Tie the angel around the neck to the end of the ribbon.

Hang the paper roll up and let this little angel help you remember all the things you want to do to get ready for Christmas.

Christmas is a time
to cook special treats.

Magi Recipe Holder

you need:

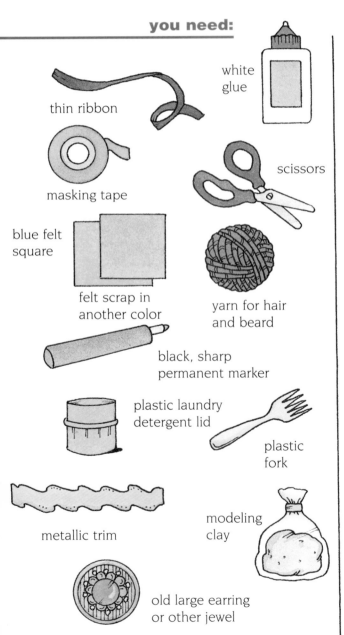

thin ribbon

masking tape

blue felt square

felt scrap in another color

metallic trim

plastic laundry detergent lid

old large earring or other jewel

white glue

scissors

yarn for hair and beard

black, sharp permanent marker

plastic fork

modeling clay

what you do:

1 Fill the plastic cap with modeling clay. Stand the handle of the fork in the clay so that it sticks straight up. The prongs of the fork will be the crown of the king and also serve as a holder for a recipe card.

2 Wrap the base of the fork with masking tape for the face of the king. Use the marker to draw the facial features on the tape on the bottom side of the fork.

3 Weave three rows of thin ribbon in and out through the prongs of the fork to form the base of the crown. Tie the two ends of the ribbon together when finished to hold it in place.

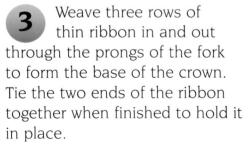

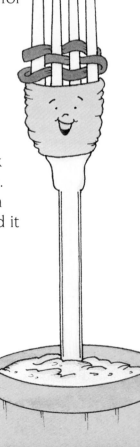

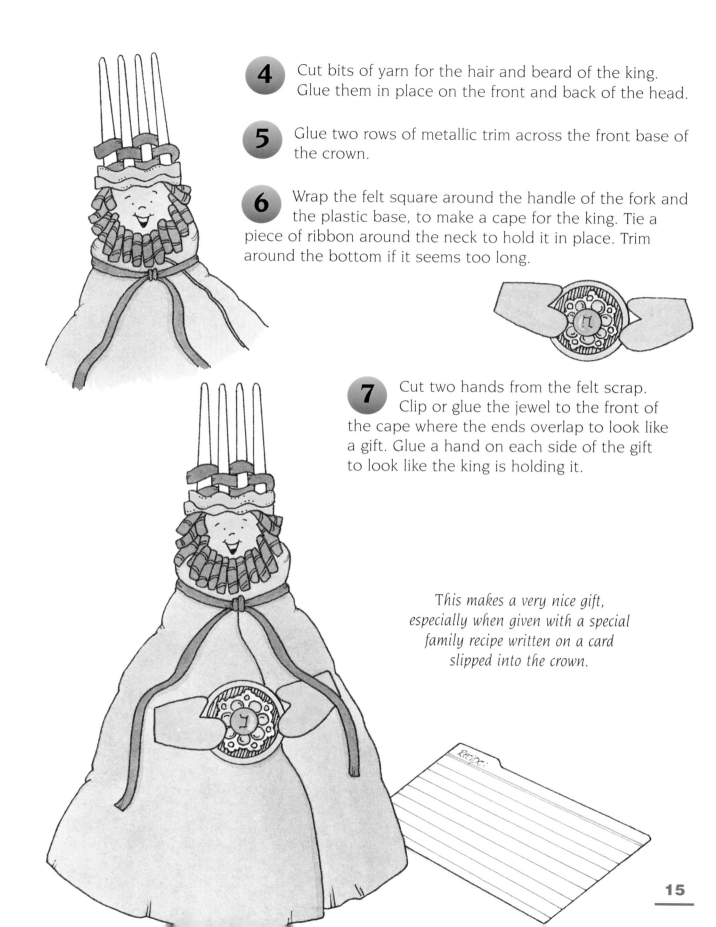

4 Cut bits of yarn for the hair and beard of the king. Glue them in place on the front and back of the head.

5 Glue two rows of metallic trim across the front base of the crown.

6 Wrap the felt square around the handle of the fork and the plastic base, to make a cape for the king. Tie a piece of ribbon around the neck to hold it in place. Trim around the bottom if it seems too long.

7 Cut two hands from the felt scrap. Clip or glue the jewel to the front of the cape where the ends overlap to look like a gift. Glue a hand on each side of the gift to look like the king is holding it.

This makes a very nice gift, especially when given with a special family recipe written on a card slipped into the crown.

Recipe:

Exchanging greeting cards is a welcome part of the Christmas celebration.

Joyful Card Holder

you need:

green plastic berry basket

two red 12-inch (30-cm) pipe cleaners

scissors

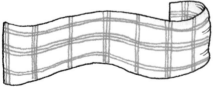

red plaid ribbon

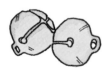

eight jingle bells

what you do:

1 Cut out two opposite sides of the basket to remove them, leaving the corner supports intact. Cut the basket in half across the bottom. Overlap the two bottom pieces to make the card holder.

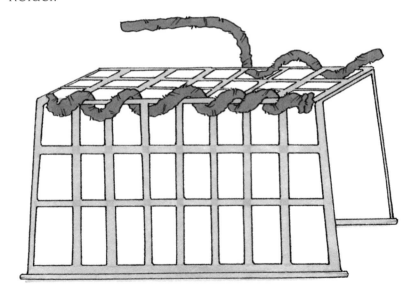

2 Cut the two pipe cleaners in half to get four pieces. Wind the end of one piece around one end of the bottom of one side of the holder. Weave the pipe cleaner in and out of the spaces on that side to sew the two pieces together. Wind the second end of the pipe cleaner around the basket to secure it. Do the same thing on the other side of the holder.

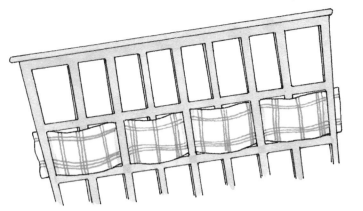

3 Weave a piece of ribbon through the open weave of the basket on each side of the holder. Trim the ends even with the sides of the holder.

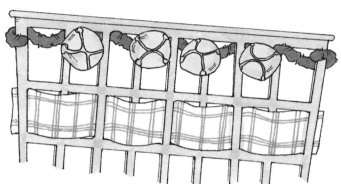

4 Secure the end of a pipe cleaner to one side of the top of the holder. Weave the pipe cleaner in and out of the basket, stringing jingle bells on as you go. Wrap the second end around the side of the holder to secure it. Do the same thing to decorate the other side.

This pretty card holder will work best when placed against a wall for extra support.

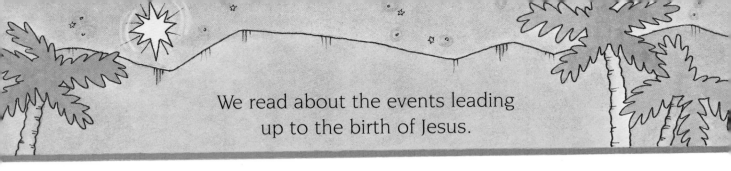

Bible Ornament

you need:

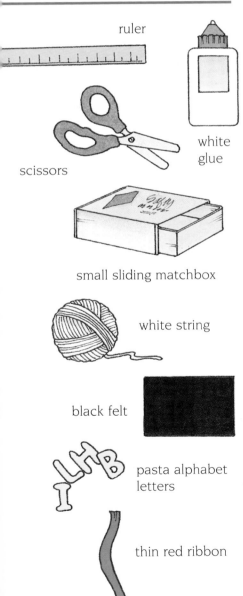

ruler

white glue

scissors

small sliding matchbox

white string

black felt

pasta alphabet letters

thin red ribbon

what you do:

1 To make the book cover, cut one long side out of the outer box of the matchbox.

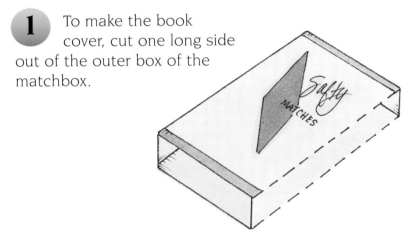

2 Cut a piece of black felt to cover the outer piece and hang over the edge about 1/4 inch (0.5 cm). Round off the corners. Glue the felt over the outer box to look like the black book cover of a Bible.

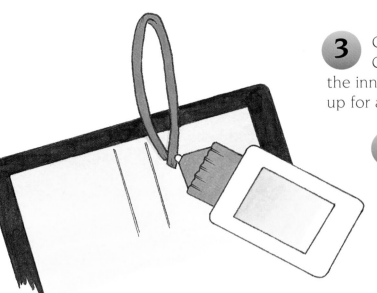

3 Cut a 4-inch (10-cm) length of red ribbon. Glue the two ends into the top corner of the inner box with the loop of the ribbon sticking up for a hanger for the ornament.

4 Glue the inner box inside the outer cover.

5 Find the pasta letters to spell "Holy Bible." Glue the letters to the front cover of the book.

6 Cut 8 to 10 pieces of white string long enough to go around the three exposed edges of the inner box. Glue the strings, side by side, around the box edge to look like the pages of a book.

What a nice little reminder to read about the birth of Jesus.

People sing about the coming of Jesus.

Joy to the World Magnet

you need:

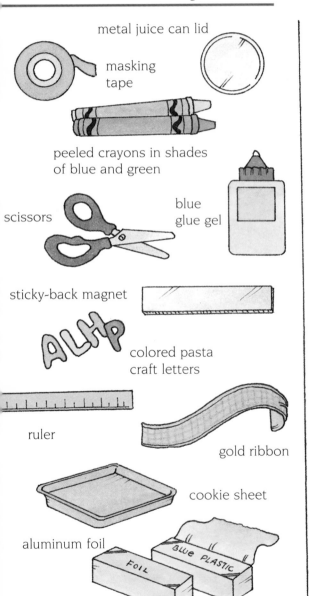

metal juice can lid

masking tape

peeled crayons in shades of blue and green

scissors

blue glue gel

sticky-back magnet

ALHp

colored pasta craft letters

ruler

gold ribbon

cookie sheet

aluminum foil

FOIL   BLUE PLASTIC

blue or clear plastic wrap

what you do:

1 Cover the cookie sheet with foil to protect it. Put the lid on the foil and cover the lid with pieces of blue crayon. This will be the water on the earth. Put green crayon on top of the blue crayon at the center part of the lid to look like the land on the earth.

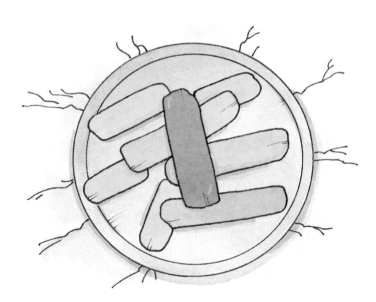

2 Ask a grown-up to put the lid in a 350-degree oven for two minutes to melt the crayon. After the grown-up removes the project from the oven, let it cool for a few minutes to harden.

3 Find the letters to spell "Joy to the World." Squeeze a line of glue gel on the front of the world for each word. Glue the letters in place. When the glue dries, the letters will not be stuck to the melted crayon background, but they will be stuck together to spell each word.

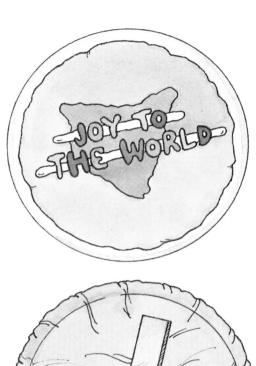

4 Arrange the words on the front of the world. Cut a 4-inch (10-cm) square of plastic wrap. Wrap the world tightly in the wrap to hold the words in place. Secure the wrap at the back of the world with masking tape and add the strip of sticky-back magnet, which will also help to hold the wrap in place.

5 Put a tiny piece of masking tape at the top of the world. Cut an 8-inch (20-cm) length of ribbon. Tie the ribbon in a bow and trim the ends. Glue the bow to the top of the world.

"Joy to world, the Lord is come."

Decorations make our homes
look special for Christmas.

Potpourri Wreath

you need:

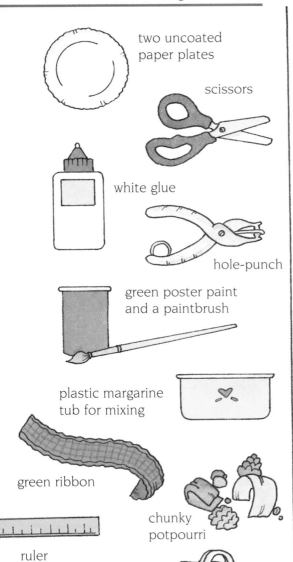

two uncoated
paper plates

scissors

white glue

hole-punch

green poster paint
and a paintbrush

plastic margarine
tub for mixing

green ribbon

chunky
potpourri

ruler

plastic grocery
bag to work on

what you do:

1 Stack the two paper plates and cut the centers out to make a wreath shape. Glue the two plate rims together.

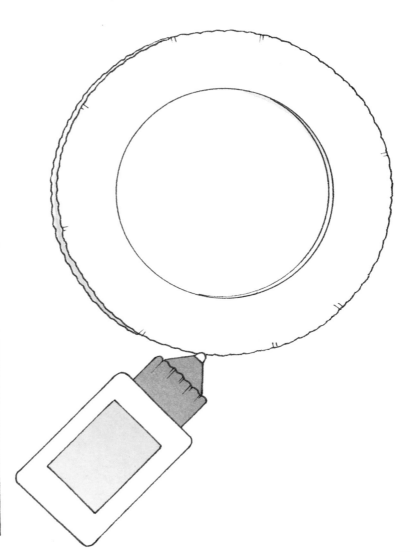

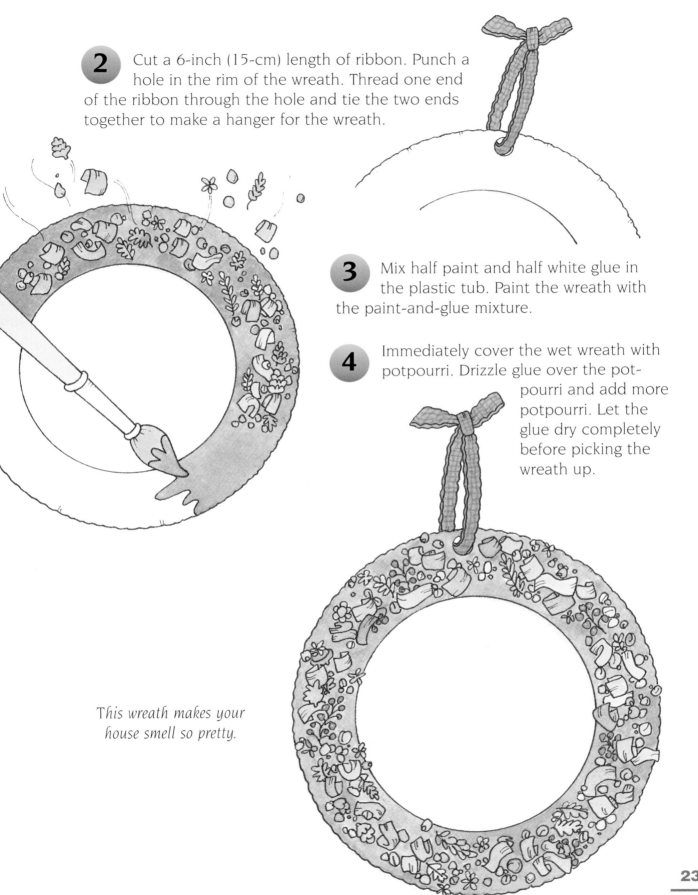

2 Cut a 6-inch (15-cm) length of ribbon. Punch a hole in the rim of the wreath. Thread one end of the ribbon through the hole and tie the two ends together to make a hanger for the wreath.

3 Mix half paint and half white glue in the plastic tub. Paint the wreath with the paint-and-glue mixture.

4 Immediately cover the wet wreath with potpourri. Drizzle glue over the potpourri and add more potpourri. Let the glue dry completely before picking the wreath up.

This wreath makes your house smell so pretty.

Candles remind us that Jesus
is the light of the world.

Beaded Candleholder

you need:

cereal box
cardboard

aluminum foil

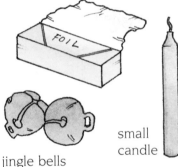

small
candle

jingle bells

pipe cleaner

ruler

beads in
Christmas colors

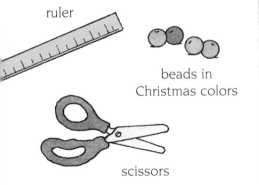

scissors

what you do:

1 Cut a 1 1/2-inch (3.75-cm) circle from the cardboard.

2 Cut a 5-inch (13-cm) square of aluminum foil.

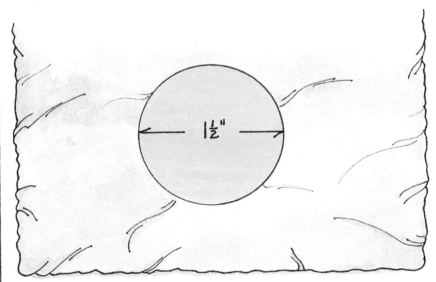

3 Put the cardboard circle in the center of the foil square.

Hold the candle in the center of the circle. Work the foil up around the cardboard circle and then up around the candle base to make a holder. Trim the top of the holder to about 1-inch (2.5-cm) tall.

4 Cut a piece of pipe cleaner just long enough to wrap around the base of your candleholder and hook together at the two ends.

5 String a pattern of beads and bells on the pipe cleaner. Wrap the pipe cleaner around the base of the candleholder and wrap the two ends of the pipe cleaner together to hold it in place.

Remember that an adult should be the only one to light a candle and to tend it while it is burning.

These candles reflect the joy of the Christmas season.

Giving gifts to each other celebrates the gift God gave to us in Jesus.

Hinge Locket

you need:

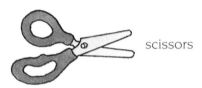

white glue

masking tape

scissors

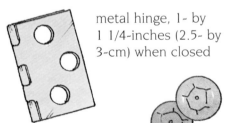

metal hinge, 1- by 1 1/4-inches (2.5- by 3-cm) when closed

large sequins

thin ribbon

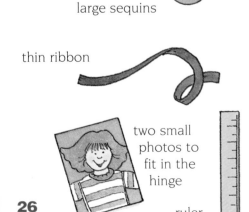

two small photos to fit in the hinge

ruler

what you do:

1 Cut each photo so that it fits exactly inside the open hinge.

2 Put masking tape on the surface of the open hinge to create a better gluing surface. Glue a photo to each side of the open hinge.

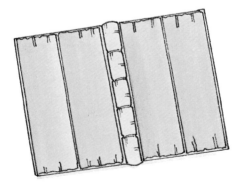

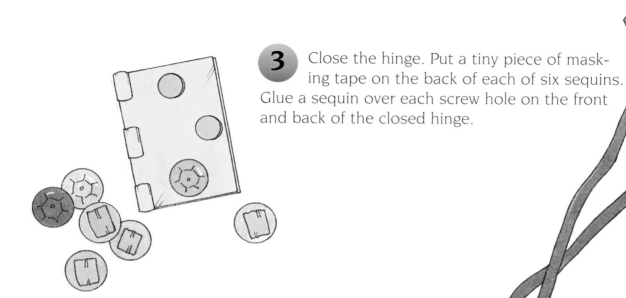

3 Close the hinge. Put a tiny piece of masking tape on the back of each of six sequins. Glue a sequin over each screw hole on the front and back of the closed hinge.

4 Cut a 2-foot (60-cm) length of ribbon. Thread one end through the center where the two sides of the hinge are connected. Tie the two ends of the ribbon together to make a necklace.

What a sweet little gift to give to someone special in your life.

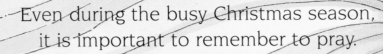

Even during the busy Christmas season,
it is important to remember to pray.

Glow-in-the-Dark Prayer Reminder

what you need:

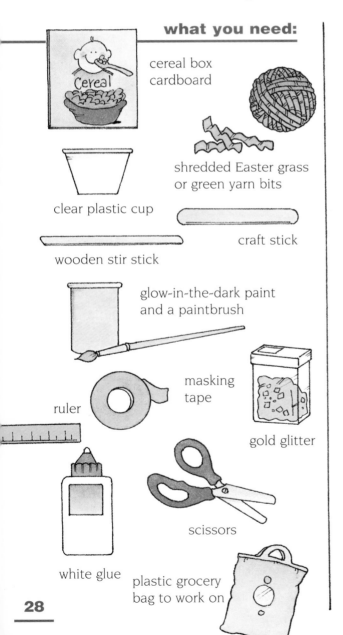

cereal box cardboard

shredded Easter grass or green yarn bits

clear plastic cup

wooden stir stick

craft stick

glow-in-the-dark paint and a paintbrush

ruler

masking tape

gold glitter

scissors

white glue

plastic grocery bag to work on

what you do:

1 Trace around the rim of the cup on the cardboard. Cut the circle out.

2 Have a grown-up use large scissors to cut a 3-inch (8-cm) piece from the stick for the base of the cross. Cut a 2-inch (5-cm) piece for the crossbar of the cross. Cut the two ends of the second stick at an angle and then glue it across the first to form the cross.

3 Secure the cross to the center of the cardboard circle using masking tape.

4 Glue shredded Easter grass around the cross to cover the cardboard base.

5 Paint both sides of the cross with a thick layer of glow-in-the-dark paint. Let the paint dry completely before continuing.

6 Cover the rim of the cup with masking tape to create a better gluing surface. Glue the cup in place over the cross, tucking the grass inside the cup. Trim off any grass that is sticking out of the base of the cup.

7 Cover the masking tape around the edge of the base of the cup with glue, then with gold glitter to completely cover it.

Put this cross beside your bed as a reminder to pray.

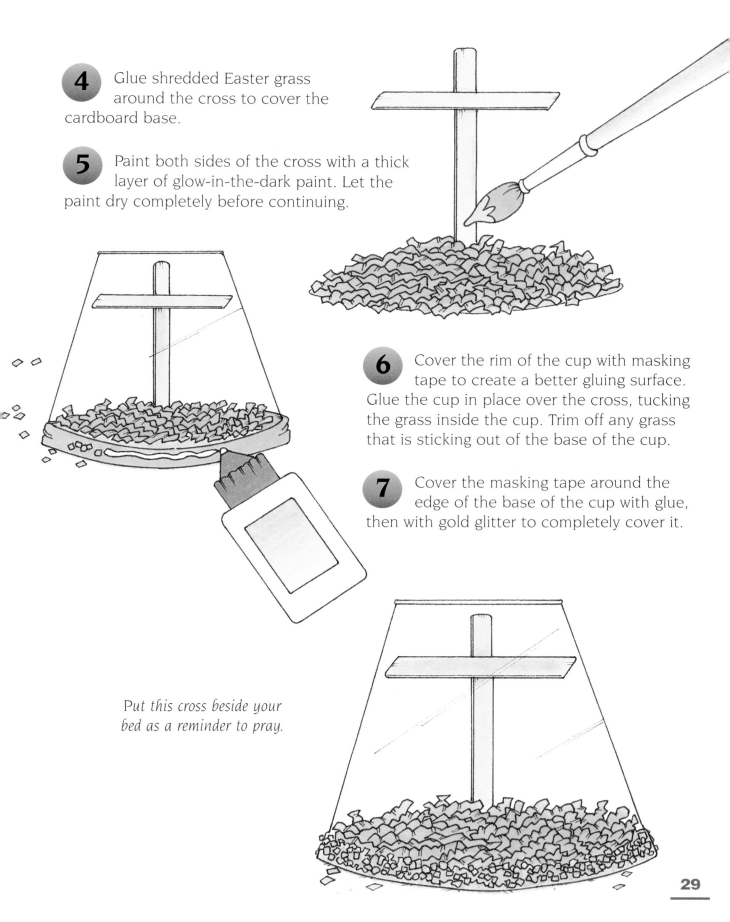

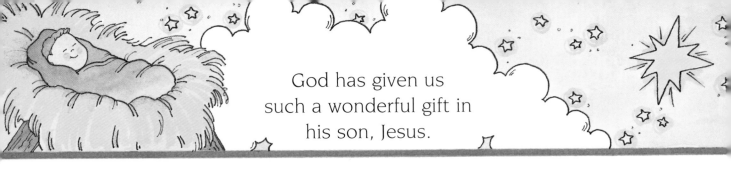

God has given us
such a wonderful gift in
his son, Jesus.

God's Gift

you need:

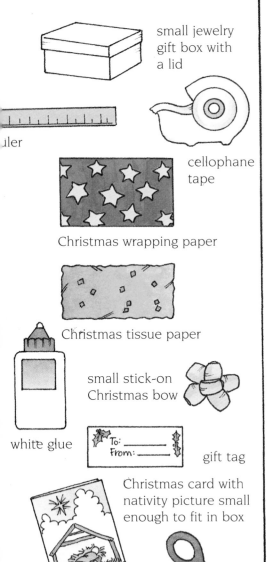

small jewelry gift box with a lid

uler

cellophane tape

Christmas wrapping paper

Christmas tissue paper

small stick-on Christmas bow

white glue

gift tag

To: _____
From: _____

Christmas card with nativity picture small enough to fit in box

scissors

what you do:

1 Wrap the lid of the box with the Christmas wrap just as you would a little package.

2 After "To:" on the gift tag write "The World." Cross out "From" and write "Love, God."

To: The World
From: Love, God

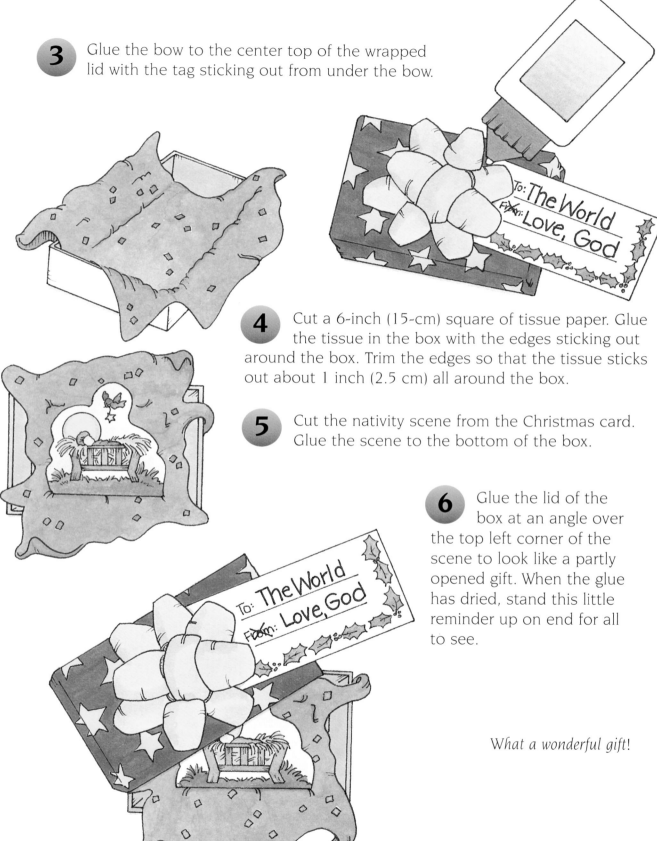

3 Glue the bow to the center top of the wrapped lid with the tag sticking out from under the bow.

4 Cut a 6-inch (15-cm) square of tissue paper. Glue the tissue in the box with the edges sticking out around the box. Trim the edges so that the tissue sticks out about 1 inch (2.5 cm) all around the box.

5 Cut the nativity scene from the Christmas card. Glue the scene to the bottom of the box.

6 Glue the lid of the box at an angle over the top left corner of the scene to look like a partly opened gift. When the glue has dried, stand this little reminder up on end for all to see.

What a wonderful gift!

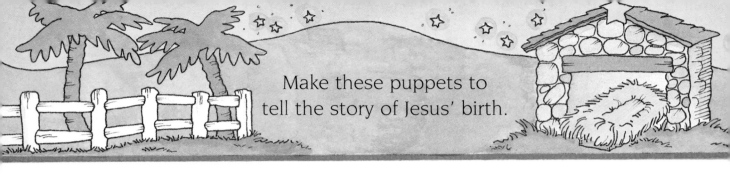

Make these puppets to tell the story of Jesus' birth.

Spoon Puppets

you need:

(for each puppet)

plastic spoon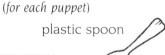

 9- by 12-inch (23- by 30-cm) sheet of construction paper

construction paper scraps in skin tone of your choice

tissue paper

masking tape

 ruler

markers

 yarn for hair

scissors

 white glue

clamp clothespins

thin ribbon

what you do:

1 Fold the sheet of construction paper lengthwise into a fan with 1-inch (2.5-cm) folds.

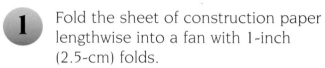

2 Cut a 3-inch (8-cm) slit down the center of the fan. Fold the two sides of the cut down on each side to form arms for the puppet and glue them to hold the fold. Use clamp clothespins to hold the paper in place while the glue dries.

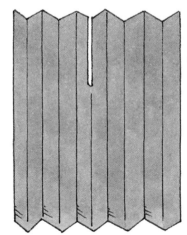 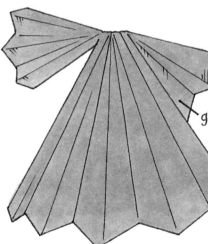

gl

3 Punch a hole through the two sides of the center-fold at the top of the dress, between the arms.

4 Cut a 1-foot (30-cm) length of ribbon. Thread an end of the ribbon through each hole from the back of the puppet and tie the ribbon in a bow.

5 Cut a 2-inch (5-cm) circle from the skin-tone paper scraps for the head. Use the markers to draw on a face. Glue on yarn bits for hair.

6 Cover the rounded back of the spoon with a piece of masking tape and glue the head to the spoon.

7 Slide the handle of the spoon through the ribbon at the neck of the dress, so the handle is behind the dress and the face is forward.

8 Give the figure a head covering by gluing on an 8-inch (20-cm) square of tissue.

To use the puppet, hold on to the handle of the spoon at the back. You can use this design to make all the adult figures in the Christmas story. Use different colors of paper, ribbon, and yarn for each figure. Make the baby Jesus by wrapping a wooden ice-cream spoon in white tissue, leaving the front of one end exposed to draw a face on with markers. You might want to glue the baby in the arms of the Mary puppet.

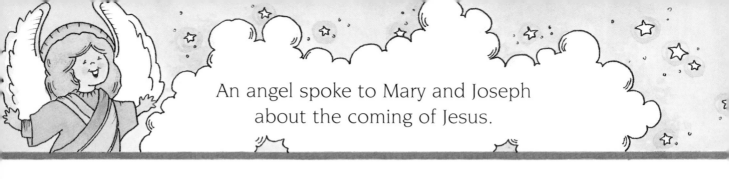

An angel spoke to Mary and Joseph about the coming of Jesus.

Ribbon Angel

you need:

spool of thin white ribbon

foil cupcake wrapper

yarn for hair

markers

1-inch (2.5-cm) wooden bead with large opening

scissors

yellow pipe cleaner

white glue

ruler

stiff cardboard

thin yellow ribbon

what you do:

1 Cut a 4-inch (10-cm) square of cardboard. Wrap the white ribbon around the cardboard 20 times, then cut the end off from the spool.

2 Cut a 5-inch (13-cm) piece of ribbon. Thread the ribbon under the wrapped ribbon at one end of the cardboard. Tie the ribbon in a knot around the wrapped ribbon. Gather it together as tight as possible. Slip the ribbon off the cardboard.

3 Cut the front and back of the wrapped ribbon apart at the bottom to make the bottom of the dress of the angel. Trim the edge to even the ends of the ribbons out.

4 Wrap more white ribbon around the cardboard square 12 times for the arms.

5 Cut two 5-inch (13-cm) pieces of white ribbon. Slide the wrapped ribbon off the cardboard and tie each end with a piece of ribbon in a knot then a bow. Cut each end of the wrapped ribbon open to make hands.

6 Draw a face with the markers on the wooden bead. Glue on yarn bits for hair. Glue the folded end of the dress up inside the hole in the bottom of the bead head.

7 Slide the ribbon arms up in between the front and back ribbons of the dress. Cut a 5-inch (13-cm) piece of ribbon. Tie it around the dress below the arms to make the waist.

8 Fold the foil cupcake wrapper in half. Cut the folded wrapper in half to make two wings for the angel. Glue the two wings on the back of the angel sticking out from each side.

9 Shape a halo for the angel from the yellow pipe cleaner with a 1-inch (2.5-cm) piece sticking down from the halo. Glue the end of the halo down in the hole in the top of the bead head.

10 Cut a 5-inch (13-cm) piece of yellow ribbon. Tie the ribbon around the base of the halo then tie the two ends together to make a hanger for the angel.

You might want to try making angels in different colors.

Animals were part of
the Christmas story, too.

Camel Gift Bag

you need:

9- by 12-inch
(23- by 30-cm)
brown padded
mailing envelope

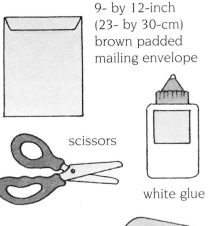

scissors

white glue

jingle bell

stapler

hole-punch

black marker

two shoulder
pads in colorful
prints

metallic ribbons
and trims

what you do:

1 Remove any labels from the side of the mailer.

2 Cut the top part of the bag off in a hump to
form the top of the camel back.

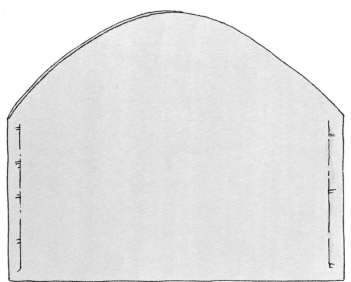

3 Cut a neck and head for the camel from the top
part of the bag that was cut off.

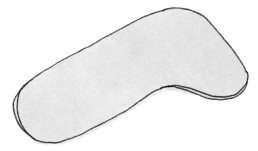

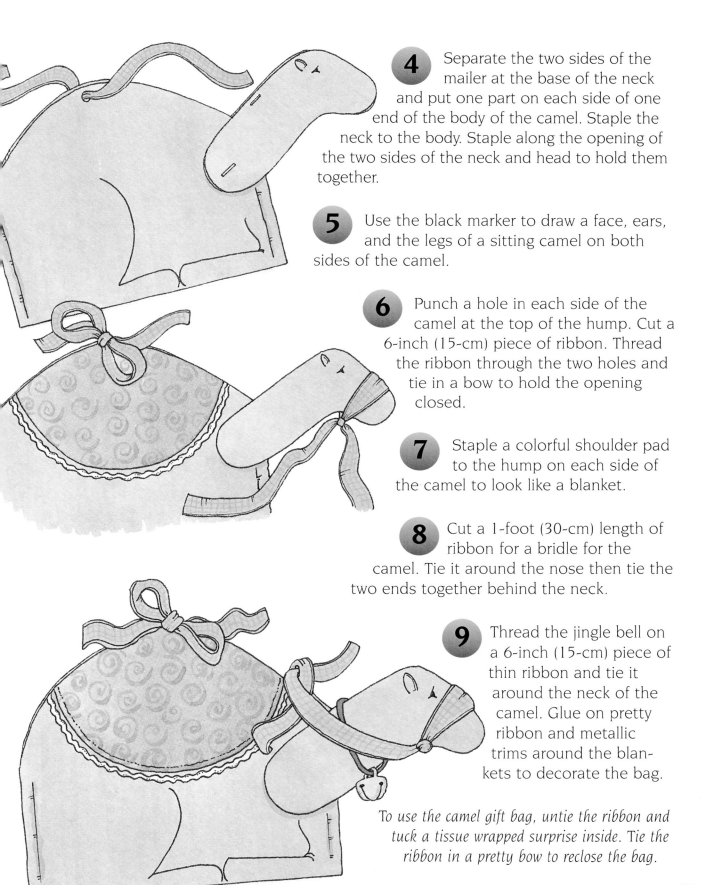

4 Separate the two sides of the mailer at the base of the neck and put one part on each side of one end of the body of the camel. Staple the neck to the body. Staple along the opening of the two sides of the neck and head to hold them together.

5 Use the black marker to draw a face, ears, and the legs of a sitting camel on both sides of the camel.

6 Punch a hole in each side of the camel at the top of the hump. Cut a 6-inch (15-cm) piece of ribbon. Thread the ribbon through the two holes and tie in a bow to hold the opening closed.

7 Staple a colorful shoulder pad to the hump on each side of the camel to look like a blanket.

8 Cut a 1-foot (30-cm) length of ribbon for a bridle for the camel. Tie it around the nose then tie the two ends together behind the neck.

9 Thread the jingle bell on a 6-inch (15-cm) piece of thin ribbon and tie it around the neck of the camel. Glue on pretty ribbon and metallic trims around the blankets to decorate the bag.

To use the camel gift bag, untie the ribbon and tuck a tissue wrapped surprise inside. Tie the ribbon in a pretty bow to reclose the bag.

Shepherds came to worship
the baby Jesus.

Woolly Sheep Ornament

you need:

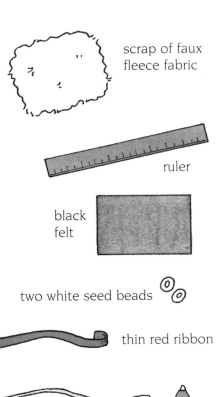

scrap of faux fleece fabric

ruler

black felt

two white seed beads

thin red ribbon

gold thread

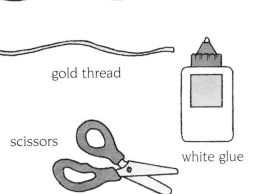

scissors

white glue

what you do:

1 Cut a 3 1/2- by 4-inch (9- by 10-cm) piece of fleece fabric. Fold the fabric in half so that it is 2 inches (5 cm) tall. Cut a piece out of the right side that is 1/2 inch (1.25 cm) wide and 1 1/2 inches (3.75 cm) long, so that a small piece is left sticking out at the top of the fold to cover the top of the head of the sheep.

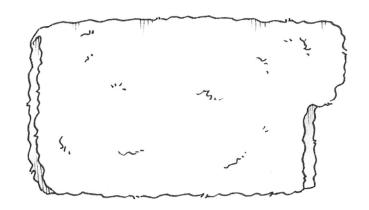

2 Cut two rectangular-shaped legs for the sheep from the black felt. Cut a third rectangle and round off its edges for the head of the sheep. Cut a thin strip of black felt and fold it in half for the tail.

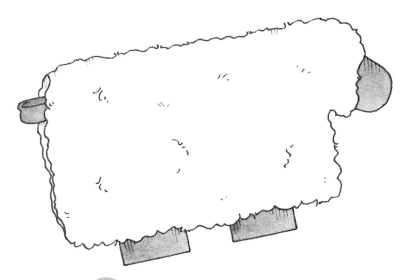

3 Open the folded fleece fabric body of the sheep and cover the inside with glue. Put the head, legs, and tail pieces in place on the back piece of the sheep body. Fold the body again and apply pressure to stick the two sides together with the felt pieces between.

4 Tie a bow of thin ribbon around the neck of the sheep.

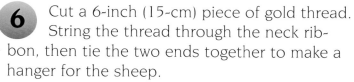

5 Glue a tiny seed bead eye on each side of the head.

6 Cut a 6-inch (15-cm) piece of gold thread. String the thread through the neck ribbon, then tie the two ends together to make a hanger for the sheep.

"While shepherds watched their flocks by night..."

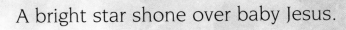

A bright star shone over baby Jesus.

Toothpick Star Ornament

5 toothpicks

gold glitter

thin ribbon

white glue

ruler

Styrofoam tray to work on

what you do:

1 Glue the five toothpicks together in the shape of a star. Make the star just as you would if you were drawing it on paper without lifting the pencil. Let the star dry undisturbed.

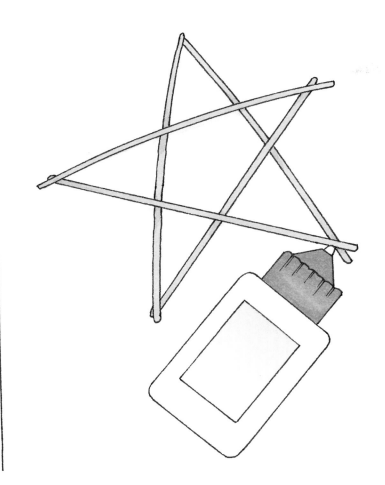

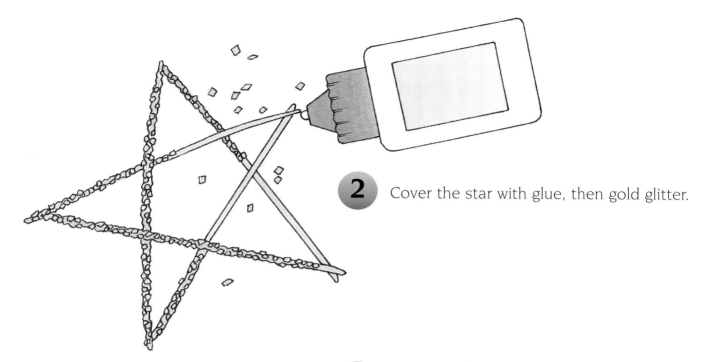

2 Cover the star with glue, then gold glitter.

3 Cut a 6-inch (15-cm) piece of ribbon. Thread one end of the ribbon through a point of the star and tie the ends together to make a hanger for the ornament.

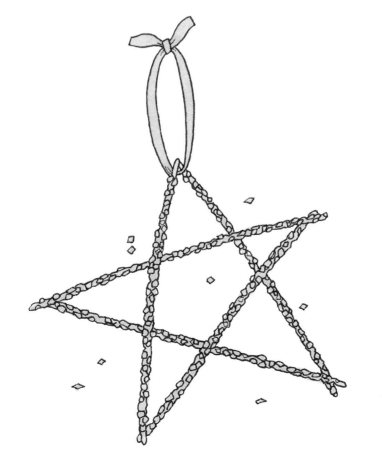

Can you shine for Jesus, too?

The three kings traveled so far
to honor Jesus.

Three Kings Banner

you need:

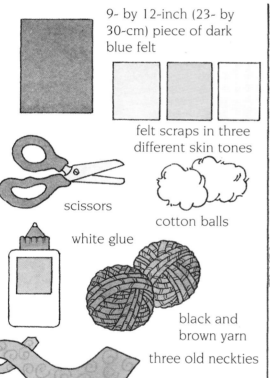

9- by 12-inch (23- by 30-cm) piece of dark blue felt

felt scraps in three different skin tones

scissors

cotton balls

white glue

black and brown yarn

three old neckties

ruler

yellow and black construction paper

gold glitter

cereal box cardboard

hole-punch

lots of different sequins, ribbons, and trims

what you do:

1 Cut a 3-inch (8-cm) circle head for each of the three kings, each from a different shade of felt.

2 Punch out eyes for each head from the black paper. Glue the eyes in place. Glue a red sequin on each head for a mouth. Use the cotton balls to give one head a beard and hair. Use a different color yarn for the beard and hair of each of the other two kings.

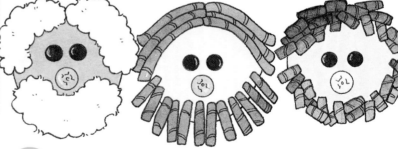

3 Cut a crown from the yellow paper for one king. Trim the crown with sequin jewels. Glue the crown on the head. Use bands of ribbon and trim to make crowns for the other two kings.

4 Cut the point off the wide end of each necktie. Cut an 8-inch (20-cm) piece off the wide end of each of the neckties for the body of each king.

5 Glue the three necktie bodies to the felt at slightly different heights. Glue a head to the top of each body.

6 Decorate the necktie bodies with sequins, trims, and glitter.

7 Rub glue around the kings and cover the glue with glitter.

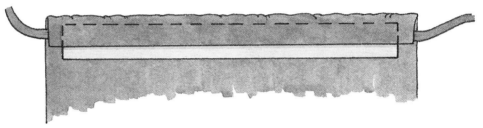

8 Cut a 9- by 1-inch (23- by 2.5-cm) strip from the cardboard. Fold the top of the banner back over the cardboard and glue it in place.

9 Cut a 2-foot (60-cm) length of ribbon. Tie the ends together to make a hanger for the banner. Slip the center part of the ribbon under the glued cardboard to secure it to the banner.

Imagine—a child so important that kings came to worship him!

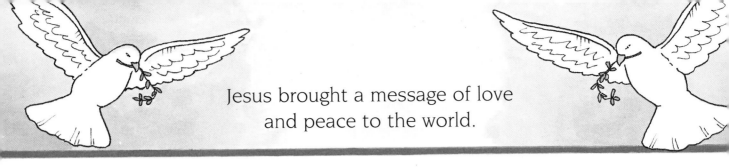

Jesus brought a message of love
and peace to the world.

Peaceful Dove Ornament

you need:

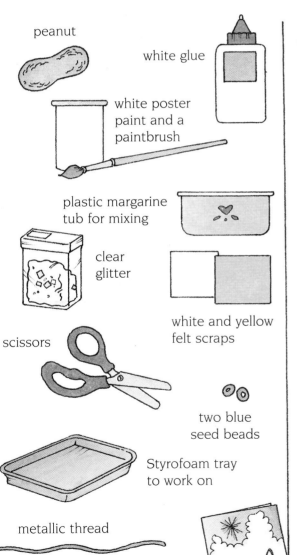

peanut

white glue

white poster
paint and a
paintbrush

plastic margarine
tub for mixing

clear
glitter

white and yellow
felt scraps

scissors

two blue
seed beads

Styrofoam tray
to work on

metallic thread

Christmas card with the
word "Peace" in the message

what you do:

1 Mix one part of white paint with one part of glue in the margarine tub. Paint the peanut white and immediately sprinkle with the clear glitter.

2 Fold the white felt in half and cut a tiny wing for the dove on the fold. Open the cut wing to get two wings. Glue the part where the two wings meet to the center of one side of the peanut.

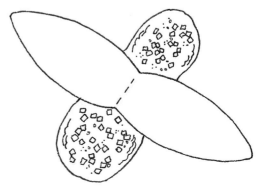

3 Cut a 6-inch (15-cm) piece of metallic thread. Tie the two ends together to make a hanger. Slip one end of the hanger under the wings to secure the hanger to the bird.

4 Cut a tail for the bird from the white felt. Glue the tail to one end of the peanut.

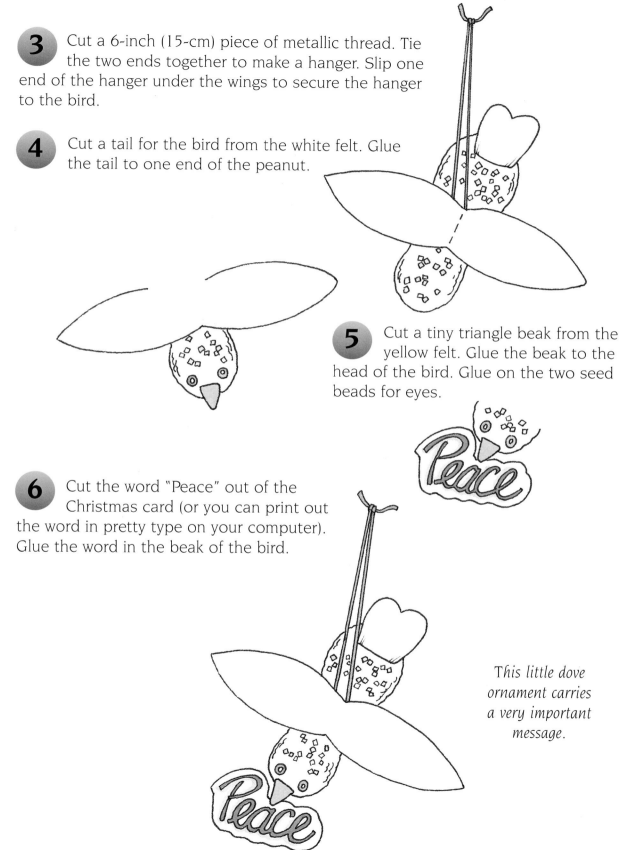

5 Cut a tiny triangle beak from the yellow felt. Glue the beak to the head of the bird. Glue on the two seed beads for eyes.

6 Cut the word "Peace" out of the Christmas card (or you can print out the word in pretty type on your computer). Glue the word in the beak of the bird.

This little dove ornament carries a very important message.

Full Heart Ornament

you need:

small sliding matchbox

gold glitter

white glue

scissors

black marker

ruler

red construction paper

Christmas card with nativity picture to fit in matchbox

pretty ribbon or trim

what you do:

1 Cut two identical 3-inch (8-cm)-high hearts from the red construction paper. Glue one heart on the front of the matchbox and the other on the back, exactly lined up with each other.

2 Use the marker to write, "My heart is full of…" on the front heart.

3 Cut the tiny picture of the nativity out of the Christmas card. Glue the picture inside the inner box of the matchbox.

4 Cut a 6-inch (15-cm) piece of ribbon for a hanger. Glue the two ends of the ribbon down the entire back of the inner box. This will make the hanger stronger than if you just glue the ends to the box.

5 Cover the inner edges of the box around the picture with glue, then sprinkle the glue with glitter.

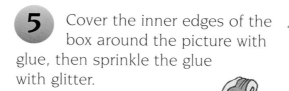

6 Cover any exposed part of the outer box with glue, then sprinkle the glue with glitter.

When the project has dried completely push the inner box back into the heart. To show what is in your heart, pull on the hanger to show the picture of the baby Jesus.

My Heart is full of...

Bible Bookmark

you need:

white envelope
with a clean
corner

blue crayon

large gold sequin or scrap of
gold wrapping paper

black marker

masking
tape

wavy-edge
scissors

ruler

star-shape punch

what you do:

1 Use the wavy-edge scissors to cut a 3-inch (8-cm) corner off the envelope.

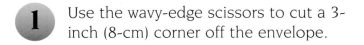
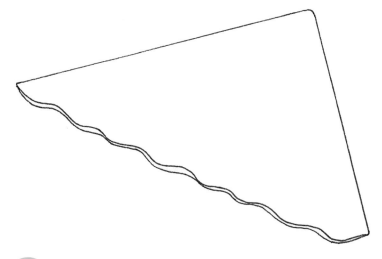

2 With the corner on the right, punch a star shape from the center of the front half. (If you don't have a star punch, you can just glue a gold star onto the project and skip the next step.)

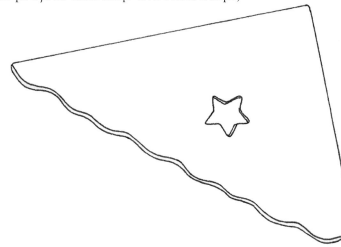

3 Use the masking tape to tape a gold sequin or a piece of gold paper behind the star.

4 Color the front of the project blue.

5 Use the black marker to write "The Birth of Jesus" on the blue space around the star.

Use the bookmark to mark the telling of the birth of Jesus in your Bible.

Some gifts can't be wrapped.

My Book of Gifts

you need:

cereal box cardboard

white glue

scissors

aluminum foil

pen

fancy ribbon

roll of adding-machine tape

ruler

masking tape

what you do:

1 Cut two 2 1/2- by 3-inch (6.25- by 8-cm) rectangles from the cardboard for the front and back cover of the book.

2 Wrap each cover in aluminum foil. Secure the folds on the backside with masking tape.

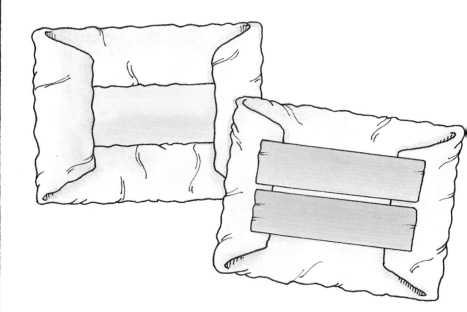

3 Cut a 2-foot (60-cm) strip of paper from the roll of adding-machine tape.

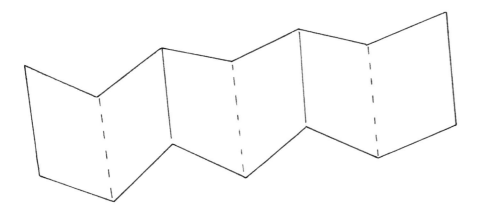

4 Fold the paper accordion-style so that it will fit between the two covers of the book. Trim off any excess paper.

5 Glue the left end of the paper to the inside of the front cover. Glue the right end of the paper to the inside of the back cover of the book. Hold the book together with the folded paper in between.

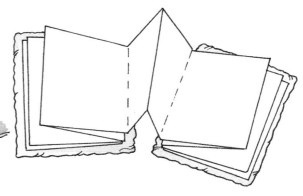

6 Put a tiny piece of masking tape in the center of the back cover of the book to create a better gluing surface.

7 Cut a 16-inch (40-cm) length of ribbon. Glue the center of the ribbon to the back of the book so that the two ends stick out on each side of the book. Tie the ends of the ribbon together in a pretty bow to make the book look like a gift. To use the book, untie the ribbon.

Use this book to write down nice things you can do for other people. An act of kindness is an important gift.

One way to show our love
and gratitude for Jesus is by
caring about others.

Prayer Necklace

you need:

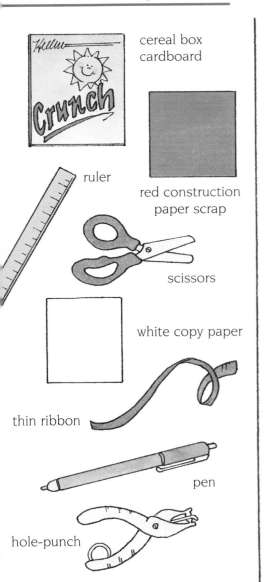

cereal box
cardboard

red construction
paper scrap

ruler

scissors

white copy paper

thin ribbon

pen

hole-punch

what you do:

1 Draw a 3-inch (8-cm)-high heart on the card-board. Cut the heart out to use as a pattern.

2 Trace the heart on the red paper. Cut the heart out.

3 Trace the heart on the white paper. Cut out eight white hearts. You can stack the paper and cut out four hearts at a time.

4 Stack all the hearts together with the red heart on the bottom.

5 Fold the stack of hearts in half to make a heart book with the red heart forming the front and back cover.

6 Punch a hole in the top center of the folded hearts. Cut a 2-foot (60-cm) length of thin ribbon. Thread one end of the ribbon through the hole and tie the two ends together to make a necklace.

7 Use the pen to write "People I am praying for" on the front of the heart book.

People I am praying for

Tammy-hurt foot

Whenever you hear of someone in need of prayer, write the name down in your little prayer book as a reminder to pray for them.

God tells us to share His love with others.

Love Notes

you need:

clamp clothespin

green marker

macaroni craft letters

white glue

scissors

red rickrack trim

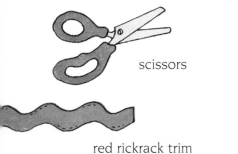
sticky-back magnet strip

what you do:

1 Color one side of the clothespin with the marker.

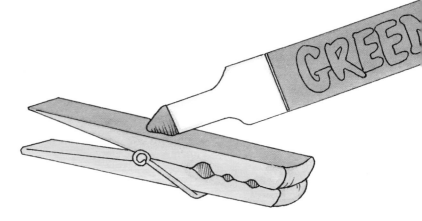

2 Cut a strip of rickrack as long as one side of the clothespin. Glue the rickrack over the colored side of the clothespin.

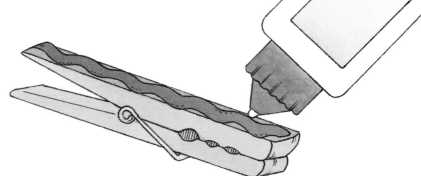

3 Find the macaroni letters to spell "Love Notes." Glue the letters down the clothespin over the rickrack.

4 Put a piece of sticky-back magnet on the back of the clothespin.

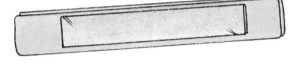

Stick the clothespin on your refrigerator. Use it to leave loving messages to the people in your family.

I love you! ☺

What fun to celebrate the joy of the season with others.

Cooperation Garland

you need:

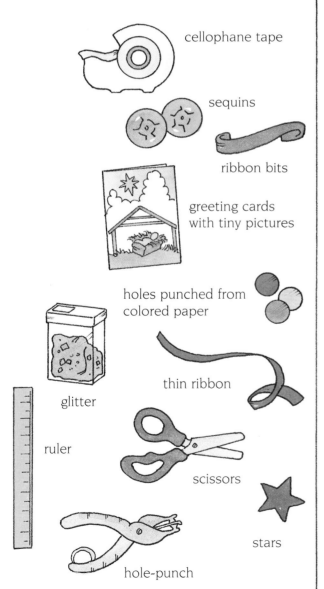

cellophane tape

sequins

ribbon bits

greeting cards
with tiny pictures

holes punched from
colored paper

glitter

thin ribbon

ruler

scissors

stars

hole-punch

what you do:

1 If this is being done as a group project, have each person contribute something different to the contents of the garland. Place all the items on the table to share with the group.

2 Tear off a 3-foot (90-cm) length of cellophane tape. This is most easily done with a friend holding one end of the long strip of tape for another person. Put the tape on a nonporous surface, sticky-side up, and turn the ends back to hold it in place while decorating.

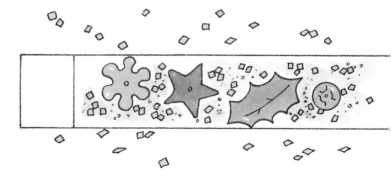

3 Sprinkle the sticky tape with a combination of the tiny collage materials.

4 Cover the tape with a second long strip of tape, placed over the first, sticky-side down. Again, this is much easier to do with the help of a friend.

5 Unstick the two ends of the tape from the work surface and trim them off.

6 Punch a hole in each end of the tape garland.

7 Cut two 1-foot (30-cm)-long pieces of ribbon. Thread a ribbon through the hole at each end of the garland, and then tie the ends of the ribbon together to make a hanger for the garland at each end.

You and your friends might have some ideas for other pretty things to put in the garlands.

Christmas gives us
so many happy memories.

Christmas Memory Book

you need:

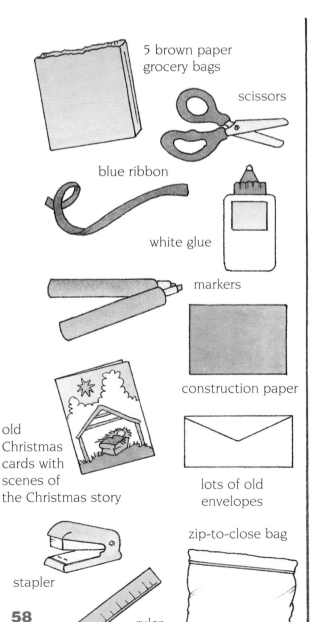

5 brown paper
grocery bags

scissors

blue ribbon

white glue

markers

construction paper

old
Christmas
cards with
scenes of
the Christmas story

lots of old
envelopes

zip-to-close bag

stapler

ruler

what you do:

1 Cut down the seam of each bag around the bottom to remove the bottoms from the bags.

2 Spread the cut bags out flat and stack them. Fold the stacked sheets in half to form a large book.

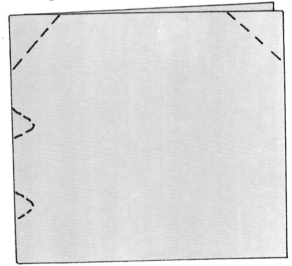

3 The front of the book will be decorated with a scene of the baby Jesus in the manger in the stable. Cut a 4-inch (10-cm) triangle off each corner at the top of the book to shape the roof of the stable.

4 Cut two small wedges out of the fold of the book.

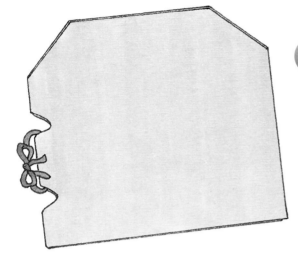

5 Cut two 6-inch (15-cm) pieces of ribbon. Thread a ribbon through each wedge-shaped hole and tie the ends in a bow to hold the book together.

6 Use markers, cut paper, and pieces cut from cards to make your own nativity scene on the front of the book. You might have some other ideas about how you want to make the scene.

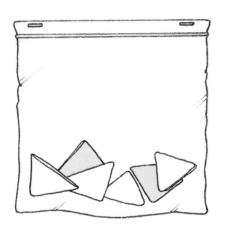

7 Cut 1-inch (2.5-cm) triangles off the bottom two corners of the envelopes. Put the clipped corners in a zip-to-close bag to save. Staple the back of the bag inside the back page of the book so that you can open the bag to get corners, then close it again to keep the extras from spilling out.

When you want to save a photo, card, program, or other item of paper in your book, slip an envelope corner on two opposite corners of the paper, or all four corners if you wish. Glue the back of the corners in the book to hold the paper in place without damaging it with tape or glue.

Fill your book with Christmas memories.

Christmas is the celebration of Jesus' birthday.

Happy Birthday, Jesus!

you need:

12- by 18-inch (30- by 46-cm) sheet of green construction paper

construction paper in your skin tone

roll of adding-machine tape

scissors

white glue

yarn in your hair color

9-inch (23-cm) uncoated paper plate

white doily

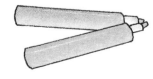
markers

ruler

white construction paper

what you do:

1 Fold the sheet of green construction paper in half lengthwise. Cut it apart on the fold.

2 Glue the two strips together to form one long strip for the arms.

3 Trace your hands on the skin-tone paper. Cut the two hand shapes out.

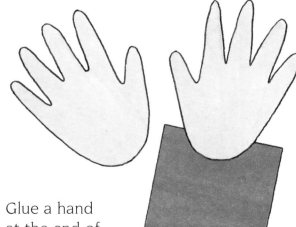

4 Glue a hand at the end of each arm.

5 From the white paper, cut cuffs for both sides of the arms and glue them on the end of each arm to cover the end of each hand.

6 Cut the doily in half. Glue the two halves to the center of the arms at an angle to make a collar.

7 Color the plate in your skin tone or leave it white. Draw on a face with the markers.

8 Cut yarn bits and glue them around the face for hair. If you are making a girl you might want to add a ribbon to the hair.

9 Glue the head to the top center of the arms with the collar under the chin portion of the paper-plate face.

10 Cut a 3-foot (90-cm) strip of adding-machine tape. Write "Happy Birthday Jesus" across the tape with markers. You might want to decorate the strip with designs or sticker stars.

11 Glue an end of the strip in each hand.

Fold the arms up to hide the paper strip. Open the arms wide to show the happy message.

This year, when you write your thank-you notes, write one to God, too.

Thank you for my family, for the blue skies.

Thank-You Note to God

you need:

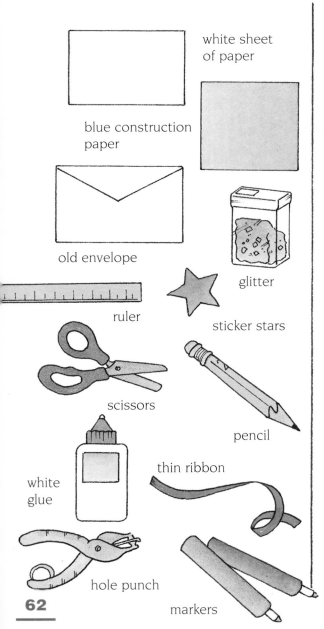

white sheet of paper

blue construction paper

old envelope

glitter

ruler

sticker stars

scissors

pencil

white glue

thin ribbon

hole punch

markers

what you do:

1 Carefully unglue the envelope to use as a pattern to make your own envelope. Trace around the envelope pattern on the blue paper. Cut the tracing out.

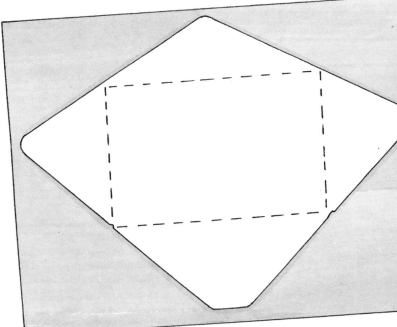

2 Fold the new envelope exactly like the one you used for a pattern. Use glue to hold the folds in place. Do not glue the envelope shut.

3 Write "To God" on the front of the envelope. On the back write "Christmas, 200_." Decorate the envelope with glitter and sticker stars.

4 On the white sheet of paper, write a letter to God that says thank-you for all the gifts of the Christmas season. Remember all the special things that you did and the special people you did them with. End your letter by saying thank-you for the gift of Jesus.

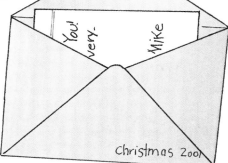

5 Fold the letter and put it in the pretty envelope you made.

6 Punch a hole in the corner of the envelope. Cut a 6-inch (15-cm) piece of ribbon. String one end of the ribbon through the hole then tie the ends together to make a hanger.

Write a thank-you note to God each Christmas. Keep the letters with your Christmas things to hang on the tree each year. Fill your tree with a lifetime of thank-you notes to God.

About the Author and the Artist

Twenty-five years as a Sunday school teacher and director of nursery school programs has given Kathy Ross extensive experience in guiding young children through crafts projects. Among the more than thirty-five craft books she has written are CRAFTS FOR ALL SEASONS, THE BEST BIRTHDAY PARTIES EVER, CRAFTS FROM YOUR FAVORITE FAIRY TALES, and CRAFTS FROM YOUR FAVORITE CHILDREN'S SONGS.

Sharon Lane Holm, a resident of Fairfield, Connecticut, won awards for her work in advertising design before shifting her concentration to children's books. Her recent books include SIDEWALK GAMES AROUND THE WORLD, HAPPY BIRTHDAY, EVERYWHERE!, and HAPPY NEW YEAR, EVERYWHERE! all by Arlene Erlbach, and BEAUTIFUL BATS by Linda Glaser.

Together, Kathy Ross and Sharon Lane Holm have also created the popular *Holiday Crafts for Kids* series, *Crafts for Kids Who Are Wild About* series, as well as three earlier Christian craft books: CRAFTS FROM YOUR FAVORITE BIBLE STORIES, CRAFTS FOR CHRISTIAN VALUES, and CRAFTS TO CELEBRATE GOD'S CREATION.